FIRST TIME LEARNING
EARLY MATHS

Here's a short note for parents:

We recommend that you work through this book with your child, offering guidance and encouragement along the way.

Find a quiet place to sit, preferably at a table, and encourage your child to hold their pencil correctly.

Try to work at your child's pace and avoid spending too long on any one page or activity.

Most of all, emphasize the fun element of what you are doing and enjoy yourselves.

Autumn
Publishing

Get ready to count...

When we have lots of things, we like to count them!
But sometimes it's not so easy...

Octopus tried to count his
legs, but he found it was
a knotty problem.

Leopard tried to count
his spots, but it made him
see spots in front of
his eyes!

Can you help Octopus count his legs and help Leopard
count his spots? Point to the numbers and say them.

1
2
3
4
5
6
7
8
9
10

Clever me!

Buckle my shoe

Find a door sticker.

There are rhymes to help Octopus and Leopard learn to count.

Here's one of them.

1, **2**, buckle my shoe.

3, **4**, knock at the door.

5, **6**, pick up sticks.

7, **8**, lay them straight.

9, **10**, a speckled hen.

How many eggs has the speckled hen laid?

What can you see?

What can you see when you count with me?

Find a bee sticker and a star sticker.

Count up to **3** – birds in the tree.

Count up to **5** – bees in the hive.

Count up to **7** – stars in heaven.

Count up to **9** – clothes on the line.

Count **10** or more – shells on the shore.

How many shells on the shore? 11

Were there more than **10**?

I did it!

Crazy creatures

How many animals are there?
Count each line of animals and circle the correct number.

1 2 3 4 5 6 7 8 9 10

1 2 3 4 5 6 7 8 9 10

1 2 3 4 5 6 7 8 9 10

1 2 3 4 5 6 7 8 9 10

That's right!

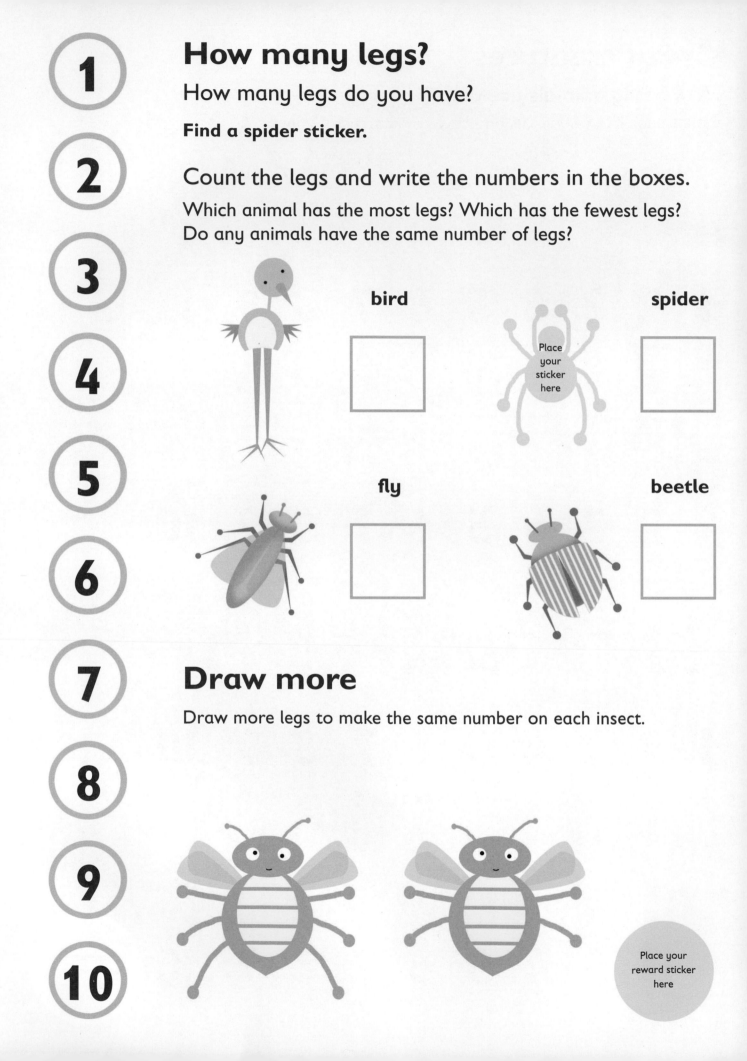

How many legs?

How many legs do you have?

Find a spider sticker.

Count the legs and write the numbers in the boxes.

Which animal has the most legs? Which has the fewest legs?
Do any animals have the same number of legs?

bird

spider

Place your sticker here

fly

beetle

Draw more

Draw more legs to make the same number on each insect.

Counting down

Write the missing numbers for the countdown from **10** to **1**.

10
9
( )
7
6
( )
4
3
( )
1

BLAST OFF!

Look again!

Here are some dots. Can you count them?

Now count these. Are there more, less or the same number as above?

Which set of dots was easier to count?
Counting is easier when things are in rows.

Look and guess

Look at each set of shapes. Guess the number in each set, then count them.

Place your reward sticker here

Number patterns

Find a diamond sticker.

Copy each pattern, then guess the number of shapes you have drawn. Write the number in the box.

Place your sticker here

Place your reward sticker here

Doodle drawings

Draw a house. Colour it in using **3** colours.

Now draw another picture of a house.
This time colour it in using **5** colours.

Find a sticker of a very colourful house.
Count all the colours you see on the house.
Write the number of colours
in the box below.

Place your
sticker here

Place your
reward sticker
here

Birds of a feather

Look at these birds. Answer the counting questions.

Find a bird sticker.

Place your sticker here

How many birds...

... have thin tails?

... have curly tails?

... have short tails?

... have bushy tails?

Place your reward sticker here

Looking at shapes

Can you make a circle shape with your hands and fingers? Can you make a triangle shape?

Here are some names for different shapes.

square   **circle**   **triangle**   **rectangle**

Shapes all around

Find a sticker of a plate. What shape is it?
Draw a line to connect the plate to the matching shape.

Place your sticker here

Find a sticker of a window. What shape is it?
Draw a line to connect the window to the matching shape.

Place your sticker here

Place your reward sticker here

Robot shapes

Find a sticker of a robot's head.

Can you see the shapes that make up the robot?

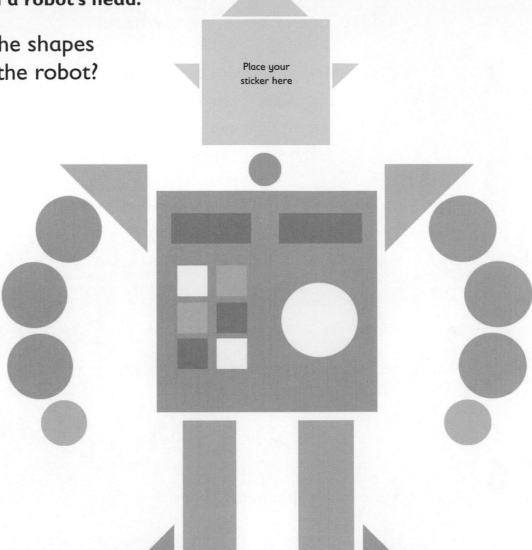

Count the shapes in the robot picture.
Write how many of each shape there are in the boxes below.
Find the missing shape stickers.

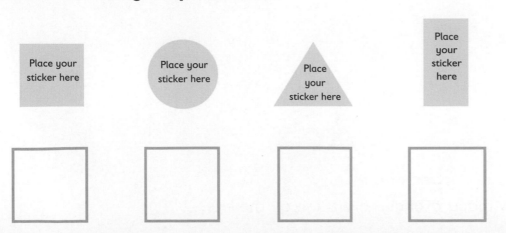

Sorting shapes

Round shapes here, square shapes there.
There are shapes everywhere!

Colour the shapes with **4** sides yellow.
Colour the shapes with **3** sides blue.
Colour the other shapes red.

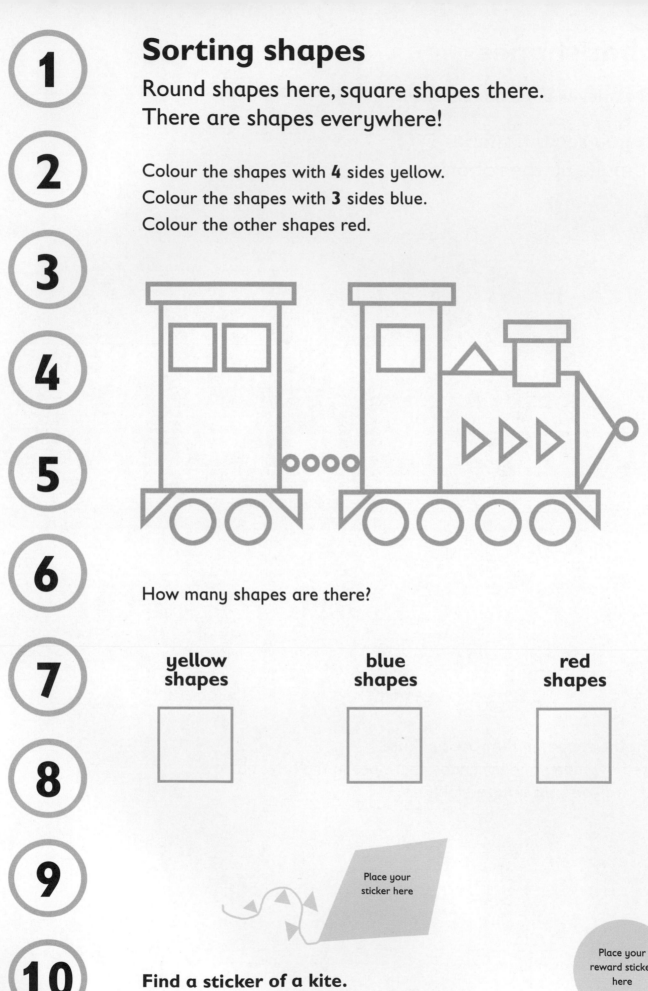

How many shapes are there?

yellow shapes	blue shapes	red shapes

Place your sticker here

Find a sticker of a kite.

How many triangles are there on the kite?

Place your reward sticker here

Terrible twins

Draw the missing shapes to make the robots the same.

Matching shapes

Colour the two shapes in each line that are exactly the same.

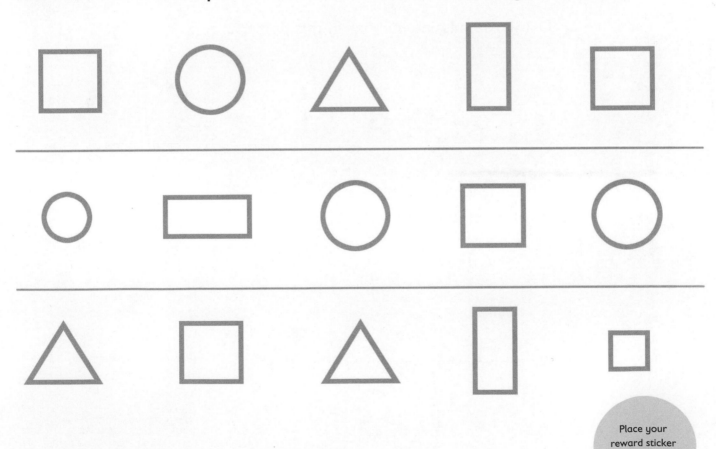

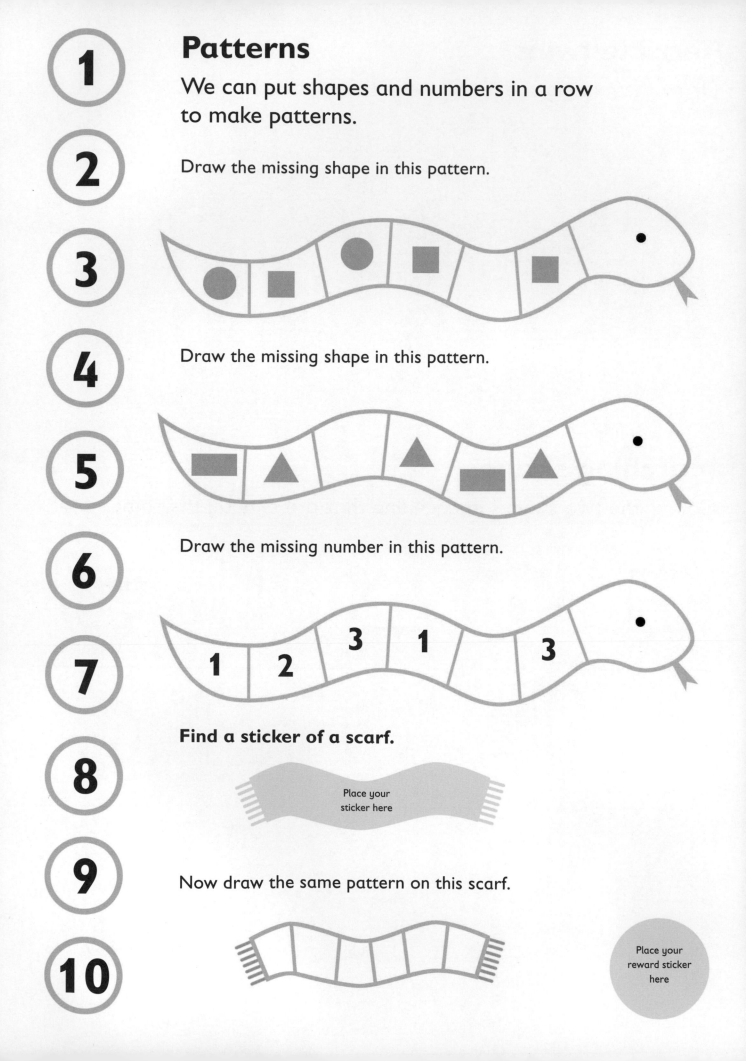

Patterns

We can put shapes and numbers in a row to make patterns.

Draw the missing shape in this pattern.

Draw the missing shape in this pattern.

Draw the missing number in this pattern.

Find a sticker of a scarf.

Place your sticker here

Now draw the same pattern on this scarf.

Place your reward sticker here

 Clever me!

 That's right!

 Well done!

 OK!

 Well done!

 I did it!

 That's right!

 Clever me!

 I did it!

 OK!

 Clever me!

 I did it!

 OK!

 Well done!

 I did it!

 That's right!

 OK!

 Well done!

 Clever me!

 Well done!

 OK!

 Clever me!

 That's right!

 OK!

 I did it!

 Well done!

 OK!

 Clever me!

 OK!

 I did it!

 That's right!

The same on both sides

Colour the butterfly's wings so that they are the same on both sides.

How many eyes does the butterfly have?

Finish the pictures

Trace the dotted lines to finish these shapes.

Place your reward sticker here

What size?

When we want to know the size of something, we measure it.

Find a sticker of a tree.
Which is the tallest tree? Colour it in.

Which is the longest log? Colour it in.

Smallest and shortest

Colour the smallest shoe.

Colour the shortest pencil.

Fitting in

Find a sticker of a cereal box.

How many cereal boxes can fit in the cupboard?
Draw them.

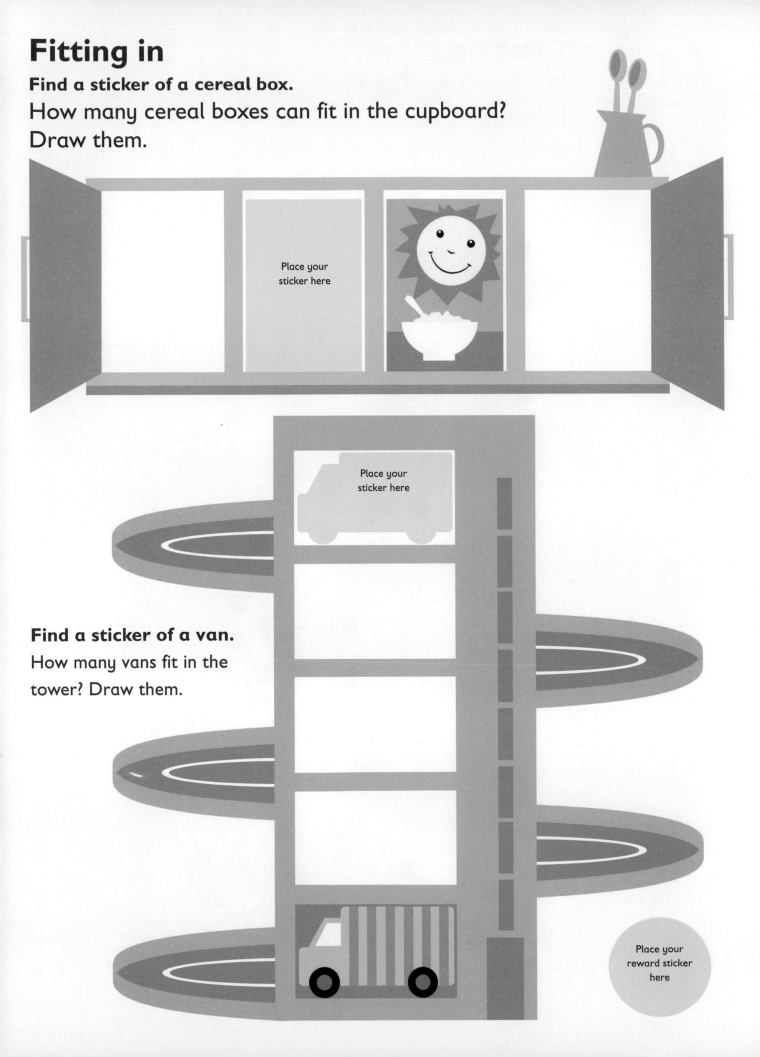

Find a sticker of a van.

How many vans fit in the
tower? Draw them.

First and last

Find the sticker of the flag to finish the picture.

In this story what picture comes first, what picture comes in the middle and what picture comes last? Write **1**, **2** and **3** in the boxes.

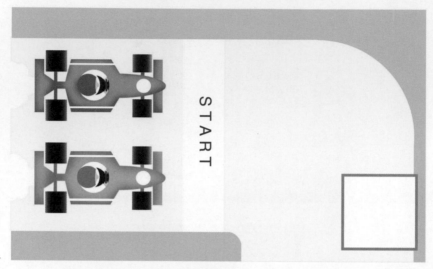

START

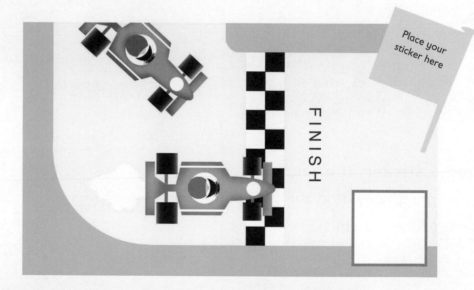

FINISH

Place your sticker here

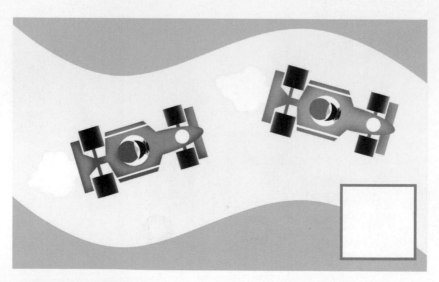

Place your reward sticker here

Long time or short time?

Find an ice cream sticker.

How long does it take to do each of these things?
Which things take a short time to do? Which take a long time?
Draw a line from each picture to the 'short time' or 'long time' box.

Watch your favourite
TV programme.

Build a house.

Sing a song.

short
time

Learn how
to be a doctor.

long
time

Grow a tree
from a seed.

Fly around
the world.

Place
your
sticker
here

Eat an
ice cream.

Place your
reward sticker
here

Draw some more

How many things are in each row? Draw **1** more.

Write the new number in the box.

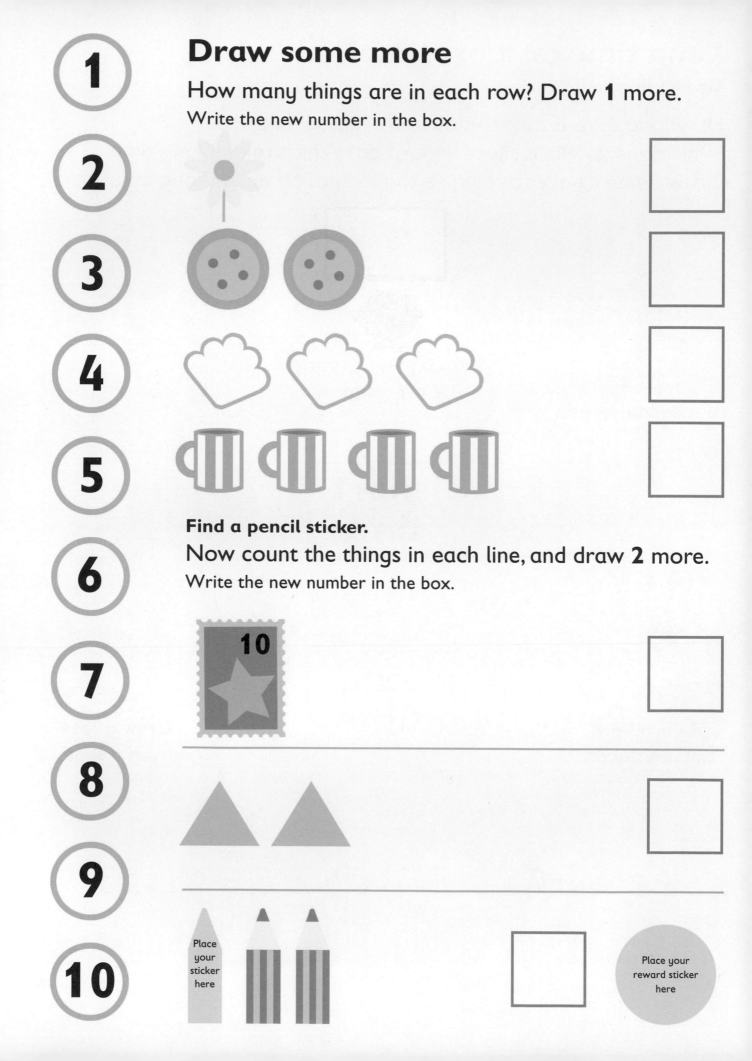

Find a pencil sticker.

Now count the things in each line, and draw **2** more.

Write the new number in the box.

Place your sticker here

Place your reward sticker here

Adding sums

Here are some adding sums for you to try.
Count the pictures in each line and write the answer.

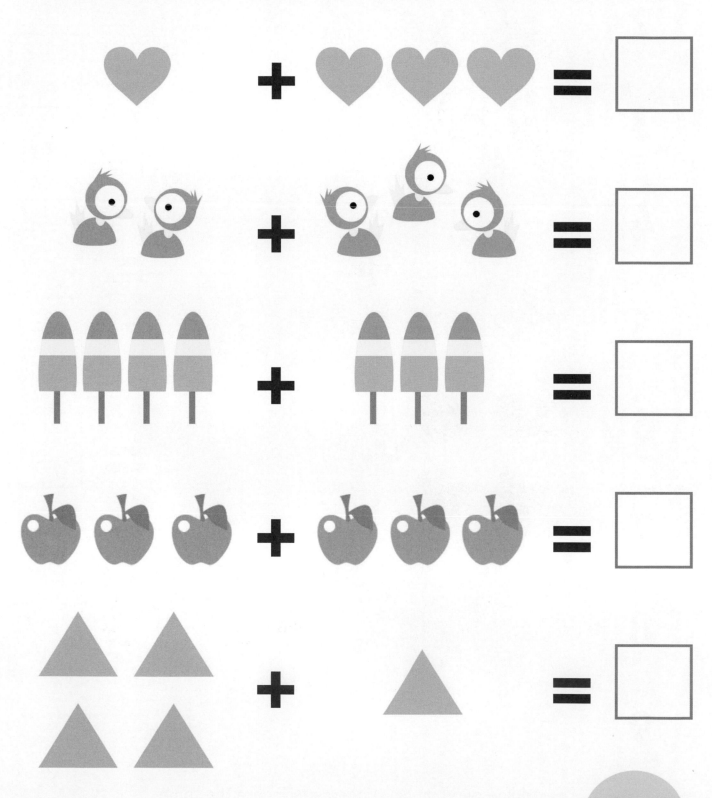

Double trouble

Find a snail sticker.

Count the things. Then draw the same number after the **+**. How many are there altogether?

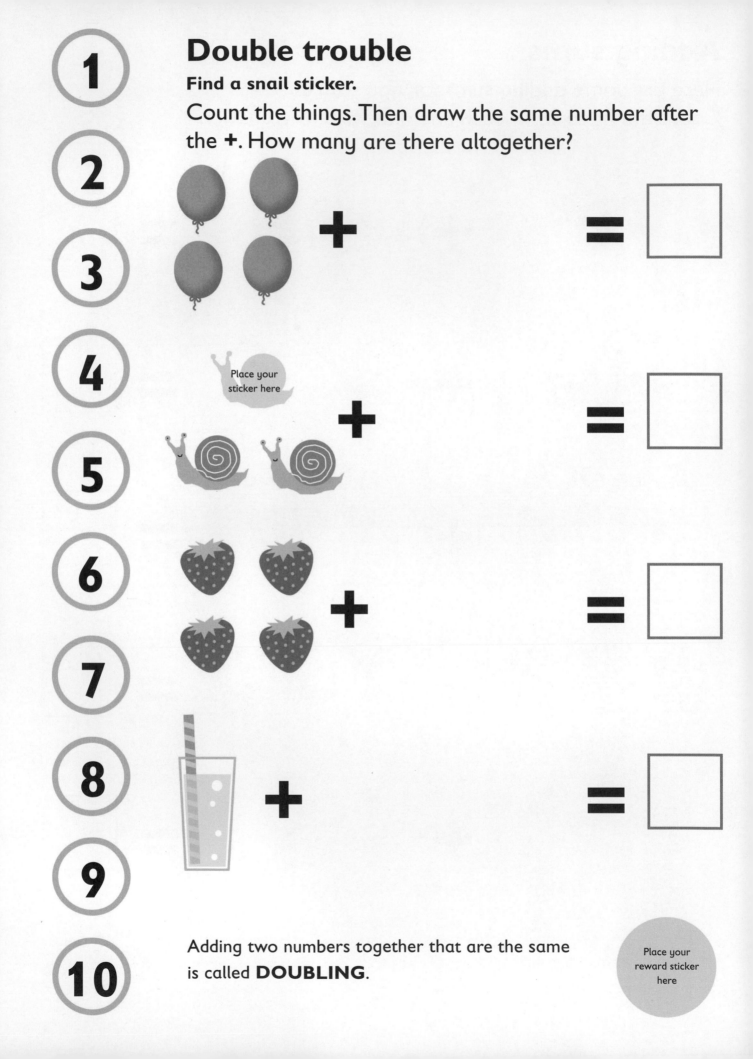

Adding two numbers together that are the same is called **DOUBLING**.

Place your reward sticker here

Making 5

How many are there altogether? Write the answers in the boxes.

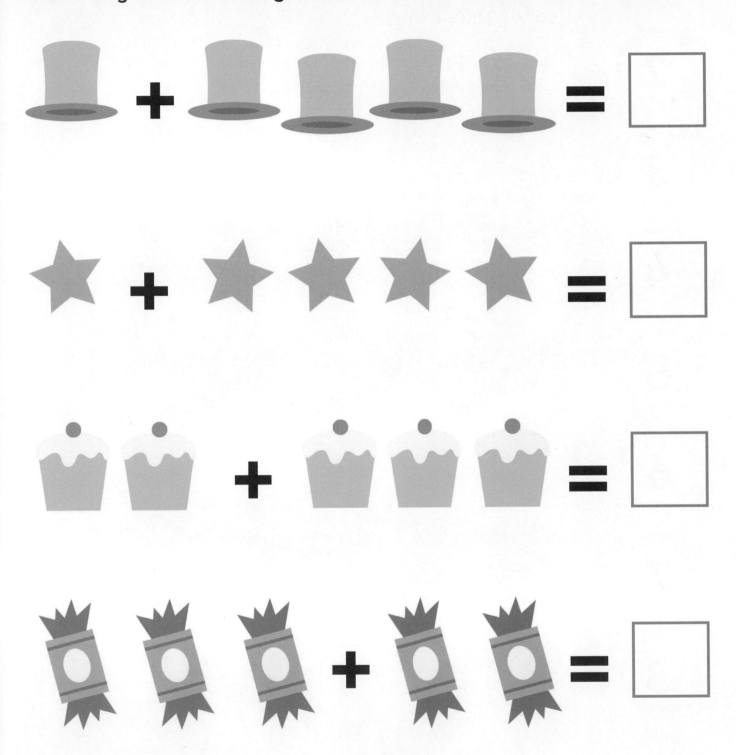

Find a rosette sticker.
The answer to these adding
sums is on the rosette.
Were your sums correct?

Place your
sticker here

Place your
reward sticker
here

Take away 1

Sometimes we want to make numbers less, so we take away.

Take away **1** thing from each line by crossing it out.
How many things are left in each line?
Write the number in the box.

Place your reward sticker here

Five teds in a bed

Find a teddy sticker.

This is a funny song. Can you learn it?

Place your
sticker here

There were **5** in the bed and the little one said,

"Roll over, roll over."

So they all rolled over and one fell out.

There were **4** in the bed and the little one said,

"Roll over, roll over."

So they all rolled over and one fell out.

There were **3** in the bed and the little one said,

"Roll over, roll over."

So they all rolled over and one fell out.

There were **2** in the bed and the little one said,

"Roll over, roll over."

So they all rolled over and one fell out.

There was **1** in the bed and the little one said,

"Goodnight!"

Place your
reward sticker
here

Take away 2

Take away **2** things from each line by crossing them out. How many are left?

When we take away things using the **—** sign, the number gets less and we have less.

Find a sticker of 2 pot plants. Can you do the sum?

Place your sticker here **—** **=**

Place your reward sticker here

Half and half

Count the objects in each line. Can you cross out **HALF** of them?
Write how many are left in the box.

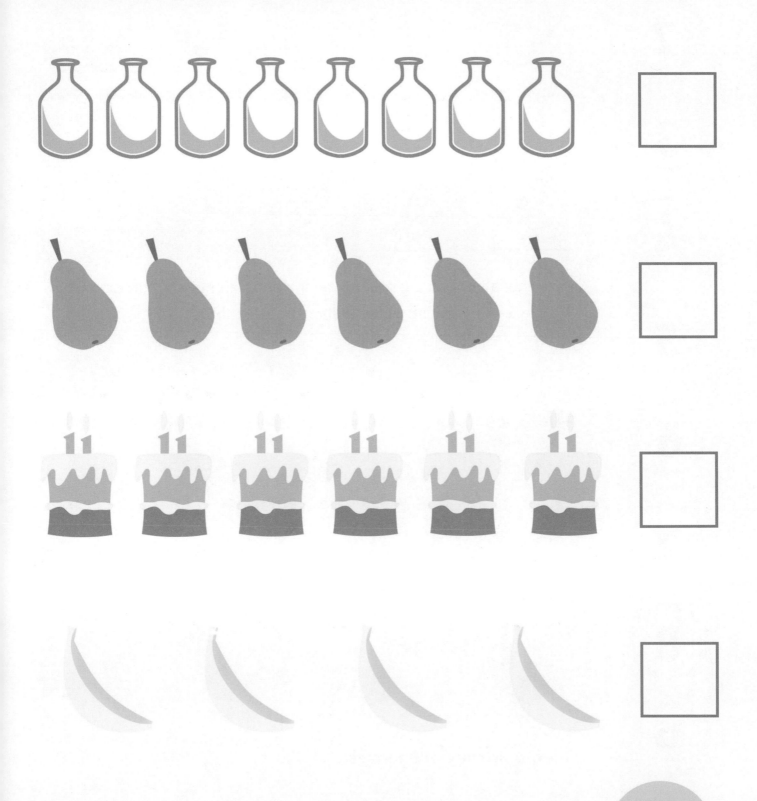

Sharing

Share out the food for the animals.

Are there enough carrots for each rabbit to have **1** each?

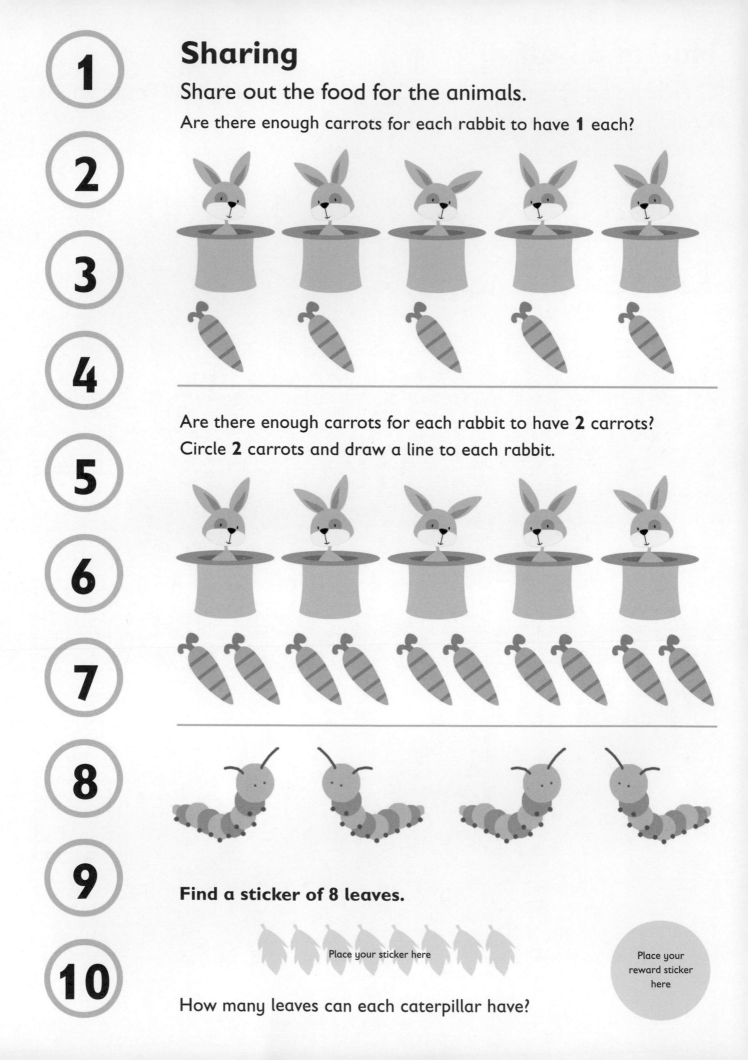

Are there enough carrots for each rabbit to have **2** carrots?
Circle **2** carrots and draw a line to each rabbit.

Find a sticker of 8 leaves.

Place your sticker here

Place your reward sticker here

How many leaves can each caterpillar have?

Share the party food

There are **3** children at a party. They have **9** sausages, **6** cakes and **3** drinks between them. How many does each child have each? Write the answers.

	drinks		cakes		sausages

Find a sticker of a sausage.

Place your sticker here

There were **10** sausages in the pack and the children ate **9**.
How many sausages were left?

Place your reward sticker here

Can you guess who ate the last sausage?

You're a star!

Find **5** triangles in the star.
Colour them yellow.

Find **1** pentagon in the star.
Colour it red.

Well done! You're a star for finishing this book!